THE ARDEN SHAKESPEARE
BOOK OF QUOTATIONS
FROM

Songs
& Sonnets

Compiled by
JANE ARMSTRONG

The Arden website is at
http://www.ardenshakespeare.com

First published 2001 by The Arden Shakespeare

Arden Shakespeare is an imprint of Thomson Learning

Thomson Learning
Berkshire House
168–173 High Holborn
London WC1V 7AA

Designed and typeset by Martin Bristow

Printed in Singapore by Seng Lee Press

British Library Cataloguing in Publication Data
A catalogue record for this book is available from the
British Library

Library of Congress Cataloguing in Publication Data
A catalogue record has been requested

ISBN 1-903436-54-0

NPN 9 8 7 6 5 4 3 2 1

Songs
& Sonnets

THE ARDEN SHAKESPEARE
BOOKS OF QUOTATIONS

Nature

Hark, hark, the lark at heaven's gate sings,
    And Phoebus gins arise,
His steeds to water at those springs
    On chaliced flowers that lies;
And winking Mary-buds begin to ope their golden eyes;
With every thing that pretty is, my lady sweet arise:
    Arise, arise!

Cymbeline 2.3.20–6

Under the greenwood tree,
    Who loves to lie with me,
And turn his merry note
    Unto the sweet bird's throat,
Come hither, come hither, come hither.
    Here shall he see
    No enemy,
But winter and rough weather.

Who doth ambition shun,
    And loves to live i'th' sun,
Seeking the food he eats,
    And pleased with what he gets,
Come hither, come hither, come hither.
    Here shall he see
    No enemy,
But winter and rough weather.

As You Like It 2.5.1–8, 35–42

When daffodils begin to peer,
    With heigh! the doxy over the dale,
Why then comes in the sweet o' the year,
    For the red blood reigns in the winter's pale.

The white sheet bleaching on the hedge,
    With hey! the sweet birds, O how they sing!
Doth set my pugging tooth an edge;
    For a quart of ale is a dish for a king.

The lark, that tirra-lirra chants,
    With heigh! with heigh! the thrush and the jay,
Are summer songs for me and my aunts,
    While we lie tumbling in the hay.

Winter's Tale 4.3.1–12

SPRING

When daisies pied and violets blue
    And lady-smocks all silver-white
And cuckoo-buds of yellow hue
    Do paint the meadows with delight,
The cuckoo then on every tree
Mocks married men; for thus sings he:
            'Cuckoo!
Cuckoo, cuckoo!' O, word of fear,
Unpleasing to a married ear.

When shepherds pipe on oaten straws
    And merry larks are ploughmen's clocks,
When turtles tread and rooks and daws,
    And maidens bleach their summer smocks,
The cuckoo then, on every tree,
Mocks married men; for thus sings he:
            'Cuckoo!
Cuckoo, cuckoo!' O, word of fear,
Unpleasing to a married ear.

Love's Labour's Lost 5.2.885–902

When icicles hang by the wall
    And Dick the shepherd blows his nail
And Tom bears logs into the hall
    And milk comes frozen home in pail,
When blood is nipped and ways be foul,
Then nightly sings the staring owl:
                    'Tu-whit, Tu-whoo!'
A merry note,
While greasy Joan doth keel the pot.

When all aloud the wind doth blow
    And coughing drowns the parson's saw
And birds sit brooding in the snow
    And Marian's nose looks red and raw,
When roasted crabs hiss in the bowl,
Then nightly sings the staring owl:
                    'Tu-whit; Tu-whoo!'
A merry note,
While greasy Joan doth keel the pot.

Love's Labour's Lost 5.2.903–20

How like a winter hath my absence been
From thee, the pleasure of the fleeting year!
What freezings have I felt, what dark days seen,
What old December's bareness everywhere!
And yet this time removed was summer's time,
The teeming autumn big with rich increase
Bearing the wanton burden of the prime,
Like widowed wombs after their lords' decease:
Yet this abundant issue seemed to me
But hope of orphans, and unfathered fruit;
For summer and his pleasures wait on thee,
And thou away, the very birds are mute;
   Or if they sing, 'tis with so dull a cheer
   That leaves look pale, dreading the winter's near.

Sonnet 97

Love

If music be the food of love, play on,
Give me excess of it.

Twelfth Night 1.1.1–2

Shall I compare thee to a summer's day?
Thou art more lovely and more temperate:
Rough winds do shake the darling buds of May,
And summer's lease hath all too short a date:
Sometime too hot the eye of heaven shines,
And often is his gold complexion dimmed;
And every fair from fair sometime declines,
By chance, or nature's changing course, untrimmed:
But thy eternal summer shall not fade,
Nor lose possession of that fair thou ow'st,
Nor shall death brag thou wander'st in his shade
When in eternal lines to time thou grow'st:
  So long as men can breathe or eyes can see,
  So long lives this, and this gives life to thee.

Sonnet 18

My mistress' eyes are nothing like the sun;
Coral is far more red than her lips' red;
If snow be white, why then her breasts are dun;
If hairs be wires, black wires grow on her head.
I have seen roses damasked, red and white,
But no such roses see I in her cheeks;
And in some perfumes is there more delight
Than in the breath that from my mistress reeks.
I love to hear her speak, yet well I know
That music hath a far more pleasing sound;
I grant I never saw a goddess go;
My mistress when she walks treads on the ground.
   And yet, by heaven, I think my love as rare
   As any she belied with false compare.

Sonnet 130

Who is Silvia? What is she
That all our swains commend her?
Holy, fair, and wise is she,
The heaven such grace did lend her,
    That she might admired be.

Is she kind as she is fair?
For beauty lives with kindness.
Love doth to her eyes repair,
To help him of his blindness;
    And, being helped, inhabits there.

Then to Silvia let us sing,
That Silvia is excelling;
She excels each mortal thing
Upon the dull earth dwelling.
    To her let us garlands bring.

Two Gentlemen of Verona 4.2.38–52

It was a lover and his lass,
    With a hey and a ho and a hey nonino,
That o'er the green corn-field did pass,
    In spring-time, the only pretty ring-time,
When birds do sing, hey ding a ding, ding,
Sweet lovers love the spring.

Between the acres of the rye,
    With a hey and a ho and a hey nonino,
These pretty country-folks would lie,
    In spring-time, the only pretty ring-time,
When birds do sing, hey ding a ding, ding,
Sweet lovers love the spring.

This carol they began that hour,
    With a hey and a ho and a hey nonino,
How that a life was but a flower,
    In spring-time, the only pretty ring-time,
When birds do sing, hey ding a ding, ding,
Sweet lovers love the spring.

And therefore take the present time,
    With a hey and a ho and a hey nonino,
For love is crowned with the prime,
    In spring-time, the only pretty ring-time,
When birds do sing, hey ding a ding, ding,
Sweet lovers love the spring.

As You Like It 5.3.15–38

Sigh no more, ladies, sigh no more,
    Men were deceivers ever:
One foot in sea, and one on shore,
    To one thing constant never.
Then sigh not so, but let them go,
    And be you blithe and bonny,
Converting all your sounds of woe
    Into Hey nonny, nonny.

Much Ado About Nothing 2.3.61–8

Take, o take those lips away
   that so sweetly were forsworn,
And those eyes, the break of day
   lights that do mislead the morn:
But my kisses bring again,
             bring again;
Seals of love, but sealed in vain,
             sealed in vain.

Measure for Measure 4.1.1–6

Tell me where is Fancy bred,
Or in the heart, or in the head?
How begot, how nourished?

It is engendered in the eyes,
With gazing fed, and Fancy dies
In the cradle where it lies.

Let us all ring Fancy's knell.
I'll begin it. Ding, dong, bell.

Merchant of Venice 3.2.63–5, 67–71

My love is as a fever, longing still
For that which longer nurseth the disease,
Feeding on that which doth preserve the ill,
Th'uncertain sickly appetite to please:
My reason, the physician to my love,
Angry that his prescriptions are not kept,
Hath left me, and I, desperate, now approve
Desire is death, which physic did except.
Past cure I am, now reason is past care,
And frantic mad with evermore unrest;
My thoughts and my discourse as madmen's are,
At random from the truth vainly expressed:
  For I have sworn thee fair, and thought thee bright,
  Who art as black as hell, as dark as night.

Sonnet 147

DESDEMONA'S WILLOW SONG

She had a song of 'willow',
An old thing 'twas, but it expressed her fortune
And she died singing it. That song tonight
Will not go from my mind.

Othello 4.3.26–9

The poor soul sat sighing by a sycamore tree,
    Sing all a green willow:
Her hand on her bosom, her head on her knee,
    Sing willow, willow, willow.
The fresh streams ran by her and murmured her moans,
    Sing willow, willow, willow:
Her salt tears fell from her and softened the stones,
    Sing willow, willow, willow.
Sing all a green willow must be my garland.

Othello 4.3.39–46, 50

How should I your true love know
    From another one?
By his cockale hat and staff
    And his sandal shoon.

He is dead and gone, lady,
    He is dead and gone,
At his head a grass-green turf,
    At his heels a stone.

Hamlet 4.5.23–6, 29–32

Tomorrow is Saint Valentine's day,
    All in the morning betime,
And I a maid at your window,
    To be your Valentine.

Then up he rose, and donned his clo'es,
    And dupped the chamber door,
Let in the maid that out a maid
    Never departed more.

Hamlet 4.5.48–55

[19]

When in disgrace with fortune and men's eyes
I all alone beweep my outcast state,
And trouble deaf heav'n with my bootless cries,
And look upon myself, and curse my fate,
Wishing me like to one more rich in hope,
Featured like him, like him with friends possessed,
Desiring this man's art and that man's scope,
With what I most enjoy contented least;
Yet in these thoughts myself almost despising,
Haply I think on thee, and then my state,
Like to the lark at break of day arising,
From sullen earth, sings hymns at heaven's gate;
   For thy sweet love remembered such wealth brings
   That then I scorn to change my state with kings.

Sonnet 29

When to the sessions of sweet silent thought
I summon up remembrance of things past,
I sigh the lack of many a thing I sought,
And with old woes new wail my dear time's waste;
Then can I drown an eye (unused to flow)
For precious friends hid in death's dateless night,
And weep afresh love's long since cancelled woe,
And moan th'expense of many a vanished sight.
Then can I grieve at grievances foregone,
And heavily from woe to woe tell o'er
The sad account of fore-bemoaned moan,
Which I new pay as if not paid before;
    But if the while I think on thee, dear friend,
    All losses are restored, and sorrows end.

Sonnet 30

O mistress mine, where are you roaming?
O stay and hear, your true love's coming,
    That can sing both high and low.
Trip no further, pretty sweeting:
Journeys end in lovers meeting,
    Every wise man's son doth know.

What is love? 'Tis not hereafter,
Present mirth hath present laughter:
    What's to come is still unsure.
In delay there lies no plenty,
Then come kiss me, sweet and twenty:
    Youth's a stuff will not endure.

Twelfth Night 2.3.39–44, 47–52

Marriage

The true concord of well-tuned sounds.

Sonnet 8

Let me not to the marriage of true minds
Admit impediments; love is not love
Which alters when it alteration finds,
Or bends with the remover to remove.
O no, it is an ever-fixed mark,
That looks on tempests and is never shaken;
It is the star to every wand'ring bark,
Whose worth's unknown, although his height be taken.
Love's not Time's fool, though rosy lips and cheeks
Within his bending sickle's compass come;
Love alters not with his brief hours and weeks,
But bears it out even to the edge of doom.
  If this be error and upon me proved,
  I never writ, nor no man ever loved.

Sonnet 116

Honour, riches, marriage-blessing,
Long continuance, and increasing,
Hourly joys be still upon you;
Juno sings her blessings on you.

Earth's increase, foison plenty,
Barns and garners never empty.
Vines with clustering bunches growing,
Plants with goodly burden bowing;
Spring come to you at the farthest,
In the very end of harvest.
Scarcity and want shall shun you,
Ceres' blessing so is on you.

Tempest 4.1.106–17

Roses, their sharp spines being gone,
Not royal in their smells alone
    But in their hue;
Maiden pinks of odour faint,
Daisiers smell-less yet most quaint,
    And sweet thyme true.

Primrose, first-born child of Ver,
Merry springtime's harbinger,
    With harebells dim,
Oxlips in their cradles growing,
Marigolds on deathbeds blowing,
    Lark's-heels trim.

All dear Nature's children sweet
Lie 'fore bride and bridegroom's feet,
    Blessing their sense.
Not an angel of the air,
Bird melodious or bird fair,
    Is absent hence.

Two Noble Kinsmen 1.1.1–18

To me, fair friend, you never can be old;
For as you were when first your eye I eyed,
Such seems your beauty still: three winters cold
Have from the forests shook three summers' pride;
Three beauteous springs to yellow autumn turned
In process of the seasons have I seen;
Three April perfumes in three hot Junes burned,
Since first I saw you fresh, which yet art green.
Ah, yet doth beauty, like a dial hand,
Steal from his figure, and no pace perceived;
So your sweet hue, which methinks still doth stand,
Hath motion, and mine eye may be deceived;
　　For fear of which, hear this, thou age unbred,
　　Ere you were born was beauty's summer dead.

Sonnet 104

Jollity

Now stand you on the top of happy hours.

Sonnet 16

Come, thou monarch of the vine,
Plumpy Bacchus with pink eyne!
In thy vats our cares be drowned;
With thy grapes our hairs be crowned.
　　Cup us till the world go round!
　　Cup us till the world go round!

Antony and Cleopatra 2.7.112–17

And let me the cannikin clink, clink,
And let me the cannikin clink.
　　A soldier's a man,
　　O, man's life's but a span,
Why then let a soldier drink!

Othello 2.3.64–8

What shall he have that killed the deer?
His leather skin and horns to wear.
Then sing him home. The rest shall bear
This burden.
Take thou no scorn to wear the horn,
It was a crest ere thou wast born.
    Thy father's father wore it,
    And thy father bore it.
The horn, the horn, the lusty horn,
Is not a thing to laugh to scorn.

As You Like It 4.2.10–19

Flout 'em and scout 'em,
And scout 'em and flout 'em,
Thought is free.

Tempest 3.2.122–4

The master, the swabber, the boatswain and I;
    The gunner and his mate,
Loved Mall, Meg, and Marian, and Margery,
    But none of us cared for Kate.
    For she had a tongue with a tang,
    Would cry to a sailor, 'Go hang!'
She loved not the savour of tar nor of pitch,
Yet a tailor might scratch her where'er she did itch.
    Then to sea, boys, and let her go hang!

Tempest 2.2.46–54

No more dams I'll make for fish,
Nor fetch in firing at requiring,
Nor scrape trenchering, nor wash dish.
    Ban' Ban' Ca-caliban,
    Has a new master, get a new man.

Tempest 2.2.177–81

Lawn as white as driven snow,
Cypress black as e'er was crow,
Gloves as sweet as damask roses,
Masks for faces and for noses:
Bugle-bracelet, necklace amber,
Perfume for a lady's chamber:
Golden quoifs and stomachers
For my lads to give their dears:
Pins, and poking-sticks of steel,
What maids lack from head to heel:
Come buy of me, come! come buy! come buy!
Buy, lads, or else your lasses cry.
Come buy!

Winter's Tale 4.4.220–32

Jog on, jog on, the foot-path way,
    And merrily hent the stile-a:
A merry heart goes all the day,
    Your sad tires in a mile-a.

Winter's Tale 4.3.121–4

Where the bee sucks, there suck I,
In a cowslip's bell I lie;
There I couch when owls do cry.
On the bat's back I do fly
After summer merrily.
Merrily, merrily, shall I live now,
Under the blossom that hangs on the bough.

Tempest 5.1.88–94

Come unto these yellow sands,
    And then take hands,
Courtsied when you have, and kissed
    The wild waves whist;
Foot it featly here and there,
And sweet sprites bear
    The burden.

Tempest 1.2.376–82

Music

Full fathom five thy father lies,
Of his bones are coral made;
Those are pearls that were his eyes,
Nothing of him that doth fade
But doth suffer a sea-change
Into something rich and strange.
Sea nymphs hourly ring his knell.
     Ding dong.
Hark, now I hear them.
     Ding dong bell.

Tempest 1.2.397–405

Music ho, music, such as charmeth sleep!

Midsummer Night's Dream 4.1.82

Orpheus, with his lute, made trees
And the mountain tops that freeze
Bow themselves, when he did sing.
To his music, plants and flowers
Ever sprung, as sun and showers
There had made a lasting spring.

Every thing that heard him play,
Even the billows of the sea,
Hung their heads and then lay by.
In sweet music is such art,
Killing care and grief of heart
Fall asleep or, hearing, die.

Henry VIII 3.1.3–14

You spotted snakes with double tongue,
Thorny hedgehogs, be not seen;
Newts and blind-worms, do no wrong,
Come not near our fairy queen.

     Philomel, with melody,
     Sing in our sweet lullaby;
     Lulla, lulla, lullaby; lulla, lulla, lullaby;
     Never harm, nor spell, nor charm,
     Come our lovely lady nigh;
     So goodnight, with lullaby.

Weaving spiders, come not here;
Hence, you long-legged spinners, hence!
Beetles black, approach not near;
Worm nor snail, do no offence.

     Philomel, with melody,
     Sing in our sweet lullaby;
     Lulla, lulla, lullaby; lulla, lulla, lullaby;
     Never harm, nor spell, nor charm,
     Come our lovely lady nigh;
     So goodnight, with lullaby.

Midsummer Night's Dream 2.2.9 ff.

This Mortal Life

Let those who are in favour with their stars
Of public honour and proud titles boast,
Whilst I, whom fortune of such triumph bars,
Unlooked for joy in that I honour most;
Great princes' favourites their fair leaves spread
But as the marigold at the sun's eye,
And in themselves their pride lies buried,
For at a frown they in their glory die.
The painful warrior famoused for worth,
After a thousand victories once foiled,
Is from the book of honour razed quite,
And all the rest forgot for which he toiled:
  Then happy I, that love and am beloved
  Where I may not remove, nor be removed.

Sonnet 25

Weary with toil, I haste me to my bed,
The dear repose for limbs with travail tired;
But then begins a journey in my head
To work my mind, when body's work's expired:
For then my thoughts, from far where I abide,
Intend a zealous pilgrimage to thee,
And keep my drooping eyelids open wide,
Looking on darkness which the blind do see;
Save that my soul's imaginary sight
Presents thy shadow to my sightless view,
Which like a jewel hung in ghastly night
Makes black night beauteous, and her old face new:
   Lo, thus by day my limbs, by night my mind,
   For thee, and for myself, no quiet find.

Sonnet 27

How can I then return in happy plight
That am debarred the benefit of rest?
When day's oppression is not eased by night,
But day by night and night by day oppressed,
And each, though enemies to either's reign,
Do in consent shake hands to torture me,
The one by toil, the other to complain
How far I toil, still farther off from thee.
I tell the day to please him, thou art bright,
And dost him grace, when clouds do blot the heaven;
So flatter I the swart-complexioned night,
When sparkling stars twire not thou gild'st the even;
  But day doth daily draw my sorrows longer,
  And night doth nightly make grief's length seem
    stronger.

Sonnet 28

Blow, blow, thou winter wind,
Thou art not so unkind
   As man's ingratitude.
Thy tooth is not so keen,
Because thou art not seen,
   Although thy breath be rude.
Heigh-ho, sing heigh-ho, unto the green holly
Most friendship is feigning, most loving mere folly.
Then heigh-ho, the holly,
   This life is most jolly.

Freeze, freeze, thou bitter sky,
That dost not bite so nigh
   As benefits forgot.
Though thou the waters warp,
Thy sting is not so sharp,
   As friend remembered not.
Heigh-ho, sing heigh-ho, unto the green holly,
Most friendship is feigning, most loving mere folly.
Then heigh-ho the holly,
   This life is most jolly.

As You Like It 2.7.174–93

They that have power to hurt, and will do none,
That do not do the thing they most do show,
Who, moving others, are themselves as stone,
Unmoved, cold, and to temptation slow:
They rightly do inherit heaven's graces,
And husband nature's riches from expense;
They are the lords and owners of their faces,
Others but stewards of their excellence.
The summer's flower is to the summer sweet,
Though to itself it only live and die,
But if that flower with base infection meet,
The basest weed outbraves his dignity:
  For sweetest things turn sourest by their deeds;
  Lilies that fester smell far worse than weeds.

Sonnet 94

Fear no more the heat o'th' sun,
    Nor the furious winter's rages,
Thou thy worldly task has done,
    Home art gone and ta'en thy wages.
Golden lads and girls all must,
As chimney-sweepers, come to dust.

Fear no more the frown o'th' great,
    Thou art past the tyrant's stroke,
Care no more to clothe and eat,
    To thee the reed is as the oak:
The sceptre, learning, physic, must
All follow this and come to dust.

Fear no more the lightning-flash.
    Nor th' all-dreaded thunder-stone.
Fear not slander, censure rash.
    Thou hast finished joy and moan.
All lovers young, all lovers must
Consign to thee and come to dust.

No exorciser harm thee!
Nor no witchcraft charm thee!
Ghost unlaid forbear thee!
Nothing ill come near thee!
Quiet consummation have,
And renowned be thy grave!

Cymbeline 4.2.258–81

Everything that grows
Holds in perfection but a little moment.

Sonnet 15

When I do count the clock that tells the time,
And see the brave day sunk in hideous night;
When I behold the violet past prime,
And sable curls all silvered o'er with white:
When lofty trees I see barren of leaves,
Which erst from heat did canopy the herd,
And summer's green all girded up in sheaves
Borne on the bier with white and bristly beard:
Then of thy beauty do I question make,
That thou among the wastes of time must go,
Since sweets and beauties do themselves forsake,
And die as fast as they see others grow,
   And nothing 'gainst time's scythe can make defence
   Save breed to brave him when he takes thee hence.

Sonnet 12

Not marble, nor the gilded monuments
Of princes, shall outlive this powerful rhyme;
But you shall shine more bright in these contents
Than unswept stone, besmeared with sluttish time.
When wasteful war shall statues overturn
And broils root out the work of masonry,
Nor Mars his sword, nor war's quick fire, shall burn
The living record of your memory:
'Gainst death, and all oblivious enmity,
Shall you pace forth; your praise shall still find room
Even in the eyes of all posterity
That wear this world out to the ending doom.
    So till the judgement that yourself arise,
    You live in this, and dwell in lovers' eyes.

Sonnet 55

Come away, come away death,
And in sad cypress let me be laid.
Fie away, fie away breath,
I am slain by a fair cruel maid:
    My shroud of white, stuck all with yew,
        O prepare it.
    My part of death no one so true
        Did share it.

Not a flower, not a flower sweet,
On my black coffin let there be strewn:
Not a friend, not a friend greet
My poor corpse, where my bones shall be thrown:
    A thousand thousand sighs to save,
        Lay me, O where
    Sad true lover never find my grave,
        To weep there.

Twelfth Night 2.4.51–66

Time will come and take my love away.
This thought is as a death, which cannot choose
But weep to have that which it fears to lose.

Sonnet 64

Since brass, nor stone, nor earth, nor boundless sea,
But sad mortality o'er-sways their power,
How with this rage shall beauty hold a plea,
Whose action is no stronger than a flower?
O how shall summer's honey breath hold out
Against the wrackful siege of batt'ring days
When rocks impregnable are not so stout,
Nor gates of steel so strong, but time decays?
O fearful meditation! Where, alack,
Shall time's best jewel from time's chest lie hid?
Or what strong hand can hold his swift foot back,
Or who his spoil o'er beauty can forbid?
  O none, unless this miracle have might:
  That in black ink my love may still shine bright.

Sonnet 65

Poor soul, the centre of my sinful earth,
Feeding these rebel powers that thee array,
Why dost thou pine within and suffer dearth,
Painting thy outward walls so costly gay?
Why so large cost, having so short a lease,
Dost thou upon thy fading mansion spend?
Shall worms, inheritors of this excess,
Eat up thy charge? Is this thy body's end?
Then soul, live thou upon thy servant's loss,
And let that pine to aggravate thy store;
Buy terms divine in selling hours of dross,
Within be fed, without be rich no more:
   So shall thou feed on death, that feeds on men,
   And death once dead, there's no more dying then.

Sonnet 146

Or I shall live, your epitaph to make;
Or you survive, when I in earth am rotten;
From hence your memory death cannot take,
Although in me each part will be forgotten.
Your name from hence immortal life shall have,
Though I, once gone, to all the world must die;
The earth can yield me but a common grave,
When you entombed in men's eyes shall lie.
Your monument shall be my gentle verse,
Which eyes not yet created shall o'er-read,
And tongues to be your being shall rehearse,
When all the breathers of this world are dead.
  You still shall live, such virtue hath my pen,
    Where breath most breathes, even in the mouths
      of men.

Sonnet 81

When that I was and a little tiny boy,
　　With hey, ho, the wind and the rain,
A foolish thing was but a toy,
　　For the rain it raineth every day.

But when I came to man's estate,
　　With hey, ho, the wind and the rain,
'Gainst knaves and thieves men shut their gate,
　　For the rain it raineth every day.

But when I came, alas, to wive,
　　With hey, ho, the wind and the rain,
By swaggering could I never thrive,
　　For the rain it raineth every day.

But when I came unto my beds,
　　With hey, ho, the wind and the rain,
With toss-pots still 'had drunken heads,
　　For the rain it raineth every day.

A great while ago the world begun,
　　With hey, ho, the wind and the rain,
But that's all one, our play is done,
　　And we'll strive to please you every day.

Twelfth Night 5.1.381–400

[48]